HAL•LEONARD

WOMEN'S EDITION
VOLUME 41

C000257727

CONTENTS

ISBN 978-1-4234-6548-5

HAL•LEONARD®
CORPORATION
7777 W. BLUEMOUND RD. P.O. BOX 13819 MILWAUKEE, WI 53213

Visit Hal Leonard Online at
www.halleonard.com

Being Alive

from COMPANY

Words and Music by Stephen Sondheim

well, some-one to pull you up short, and put you through

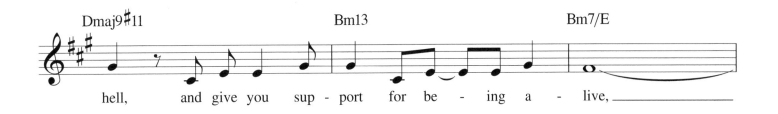

hell, and give you sup-port for be-ing a-live,

be-ing a-live. Make me a-live.

Bridge

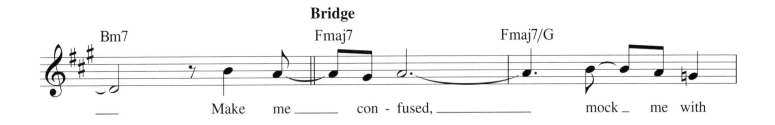

Make me con-fused, mock me with

praise. Let me be used, var-y my

days. But a-lone is a-

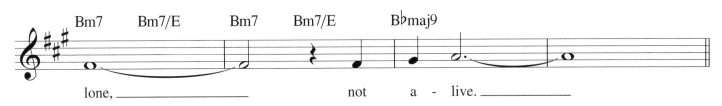

lone, not a-live.

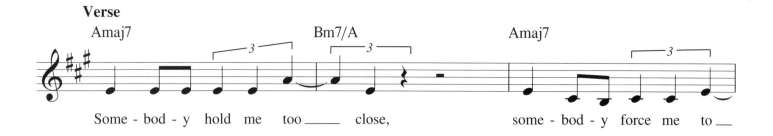

Verse

Amaj7   Bm7/A   Amaj7

Some - bod - y hold me too ____ close,   some - bod - y force me to ____

G#°7/A   Amaj7   F#m9

____ care.   Some-bod - y make me come through. I'll al - ways be

Dmaj9#11   Bm13

there,   as fright - ened as you,   of be - ing a -

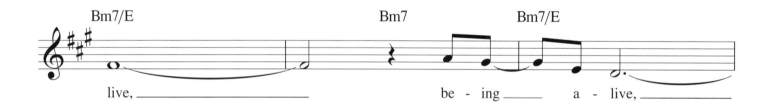

Bm7/E   Bm7   Bm7/E

live, _____   be - ing ____ a - live, ____

D#m7♭5   Dm7

____ be - ing ____ a - live. ____

Verse

Am/C   B7♭5   B♭maj7

____   Some - one you have to let ____

Cm7/B♭   B♭maj7   A°7/B♭

____ in,   some - one whose feel - ings you ____ spare,

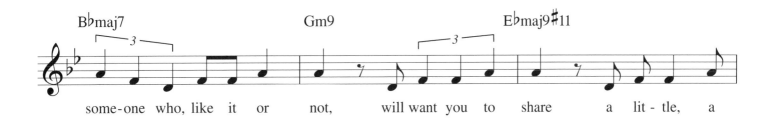

some-one who, like it or not, will want you to share a lit - tle, a

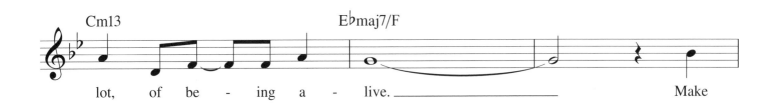

lot, of be - ing a - live. _____ Make

Bridge

me a - live. _____ Make ___ me con -

fused, _____ mock ___ me with praise.

Let me be used, ___ var - y my ___ days. _____

But a - lone _____ is a - lone, _____ not a -

Verse

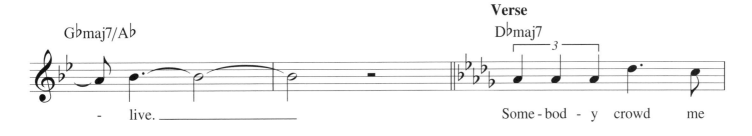

- live. _____ Some - bod - y crowd me

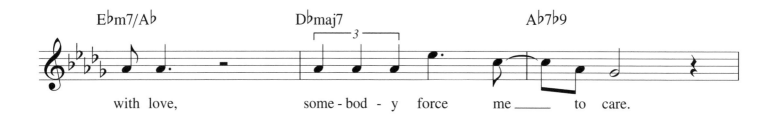

with love, some-bod-y force me _____ to care.

Some-bod-y make me come through. I'll al - ways be there, ___

___ as fright-ened as you, to help ___ us sur - vive. ___

___ Be - ing a - live, ___ be - ing a -

live, ___ be - ing a - live, ___

___ be - ing a - live. ___

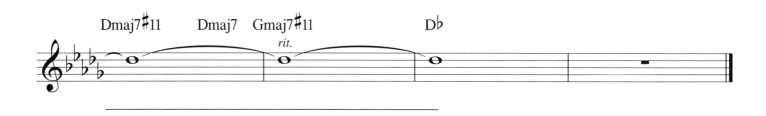

I Enjoy Being a Girl

from FLOWER DRUM SONG
Lyrics by Oscar Hammerstein II
Music by Richard Rodgers

Intro
Easy Two

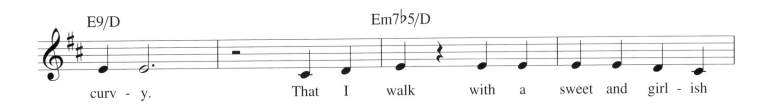

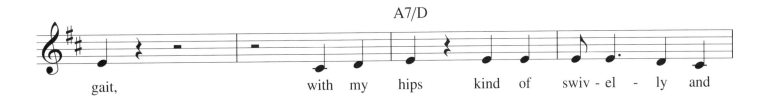

Chorus

D6   D6/9

strict - ly a fe - male fe - male, _____ and my

A7

fu - ture I hope will be in the

D/F♯   B7   Em7   E13

home of a brave and free ___ male who'll en -

D/A   Bm7   Em7   Em7♭5/B♭

joy be - ing a guy, hav - ing a

D6/A   A13

girl _____ like _____

D   Fm   A13

me. _____ When

Verse

D   D6   D6/9

men say I'm sweet as can - dy, _____ as a -

A7

round in a dance we whirl, it

10

sea,   I turn and I glow - er and I

bris - tle,   but I'm hap - py to know that

whis - tle's meant for me. _____ I'm

Outro-Chorus

strict - ly a fe - male fe - male, ____ and my

fu - ture I hope will be   in the

home of a brave and free ___ male who'll en -

joy be - ing a guy, hav - ing a

girl _____ like _____

me. _____

I've Never Been In Love Before

from GUYS AND DOLLS
By Frank Loesser

Intro
Expressively

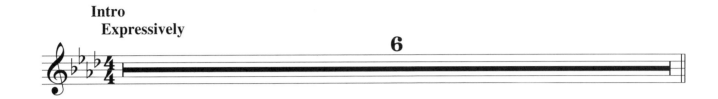

Chorus

I've nev - er been in love be - fore.

Now, all at once, it's you, it's you for - ev -

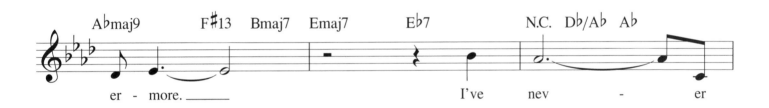

er - more. ___ I've nev - er

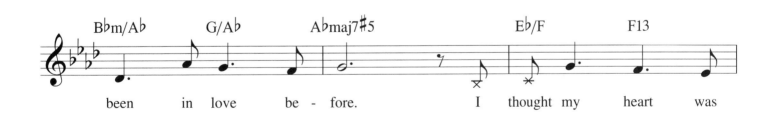

been in love be - fore. I thought my heart was

safe, I thought I knew the score. ___

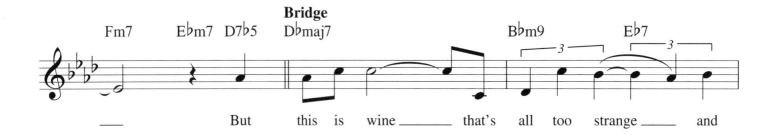

Bridge

But this is wine _____ that's all too strange _____ and

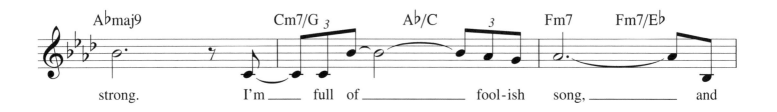

strong. I'm _____ full of _____ fool-ish song, _____ and

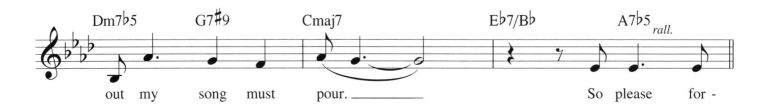

out my song must pour. _____ So please for -

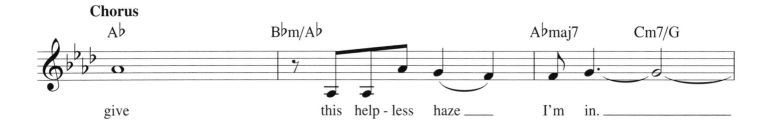

Chorus

give this help-less haze _____ I'm in. _____

_____ I've _____ nev - er real - ly been _____ in

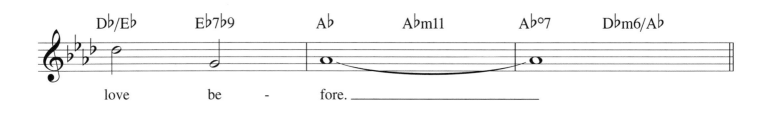

love be - fore. _____

Interlude

Luck Be a Lady

from GUYS AND DOLLS
By Frank Loesser

Intro
Freely, with motion

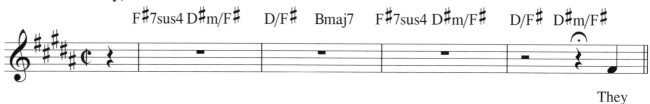

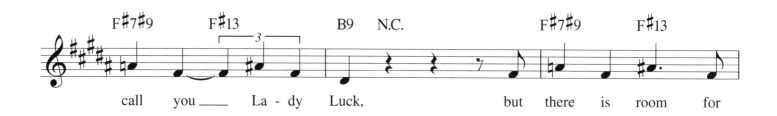

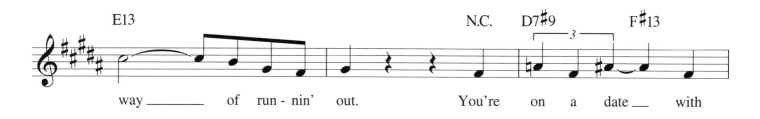

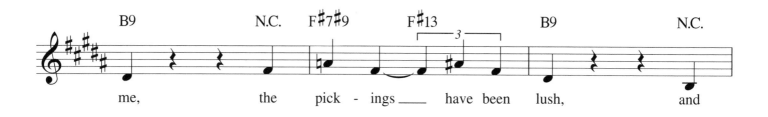

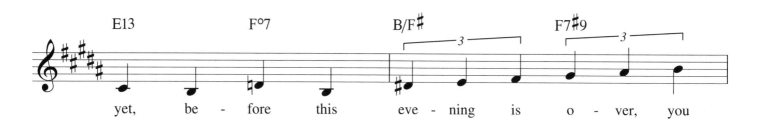

good a friend you ___ can be.

Stick with me, sis - ter, I'm the one that you came in with.

Luck be a la - dy with me. ___ The

Bridge

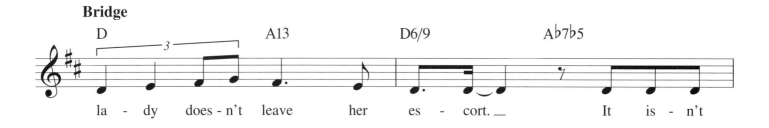

la - dy does - n't leave her es - cort. ___ It is - n't

fair, it is - n't nice. The la - dy does - n't wan - der all

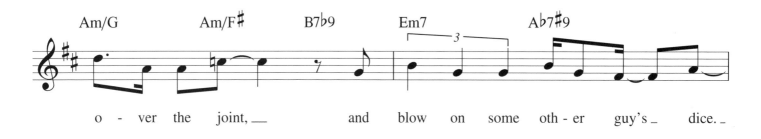

o - ver the joint, ___ and blow on some oth - er guy's ___ dice.

Chorus

___ So let's keep ___ the par - ty ___ po -

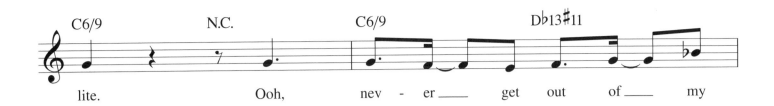

C6/9   N.C.   C6/9   Db13#11

lite.   Ooh,   nev - er ___ get out of ___ my

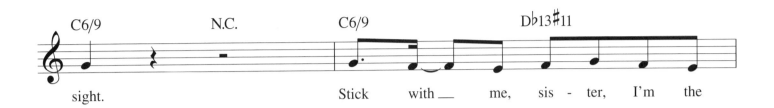

C6/9   N.C.   C6/9   Db13#11

sight.   Stick with __ me, sis - ter, I'm the

Bb7   A7   F6/9 E7#9   Eb6   D7 F2/Db   N.C.

gal that you came in with. Luck be a la - dy to - night. ___

Interlude

4   **3**

Bridge
Slower, freely

Dbadd9   A13   D   A13b9   Dmaj9   G13

rit.

The la - dy would-n't flirt with stran - gers. She'd have a

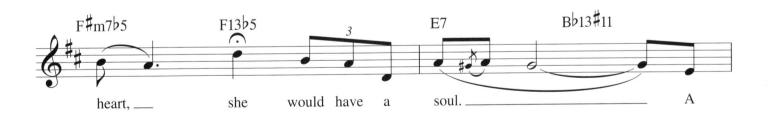

F#m7b5   F13b5   E7   Bb13#11

heart, ___ she would have a soul. _____ A

Am   F#m7b5   F13   B7b5

la - dy would - n't make lit - tle snick - ers at you when

Latin, as before

Em7   Ebm7   Am7/D   Ab7#5   N.C.   Db13#11

I bet my life on this roll. _____ So

Outro-Chorus

C6/9   Db13#11   C6/9   Db13#11

let's keep __ the par - ty __ po - lite. Nev -

C6/9   Db13#11   C6/9   Db13#11

- er __ get out of __ my sight.

Fm9   Gm7   Bb/Ab   C/Bb   Bm7b5   E7#9   Bb7   A7alt

Stick with __ me, pal, 'cause I'm the gal that you came in with.

Abmaj13   F2/Db   Cm7   F7

Luck be a la - dy, _____ oh,

Amaj13   F#2/D   Dbm7   Gb7   Bbmaj9   Abmaj9#11

luck be a la - dy, _____ luck be a

Gb6/9   Eb6/F   D7#9

la - dy _____ to -

Dbmaj13#11   C

- night. _____

The Music of the Night

from THE PHANTOM OF THE OPERA

Music by Andrew Lloyd Webber
Lyrics by Charles Hart
Additional Lyrics by Richard Stilgoe

Intro
Romantically

Verse
Slow 4

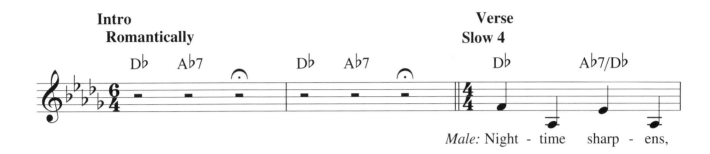

Male: Night - time sharp - ens,

height - ens each sen - sa - tion. Dark - ness stirs and

wakes i - mag - i - na - tion. Si - lent - ly the sens - es a -

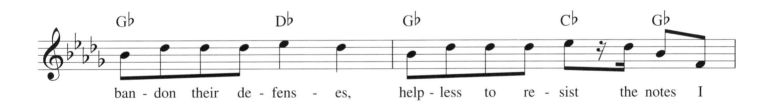

ban - don their de - fens - es, help - less to re - sist the notes I

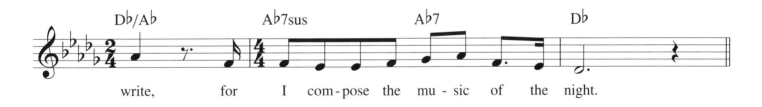

write, for I com - pose the mu - sic of the night.

Verse

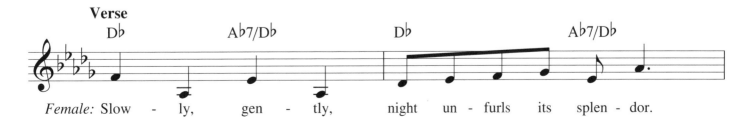

Female: Slow - ly, gen - tly, night un - furls its splen - dor.

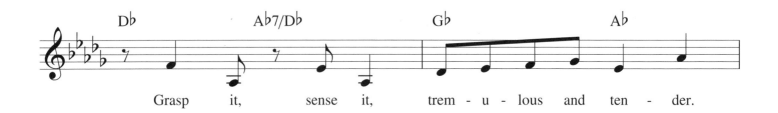

Grasp it, sense it, trem-u-lous and ten-der.

Girl: Hear-ing is be-liev-ing, mu-sic is de-ceiv-ing, _____

Guy: Hear-ing is be-liev-ing, mu-sic is de-ceiv-ing.

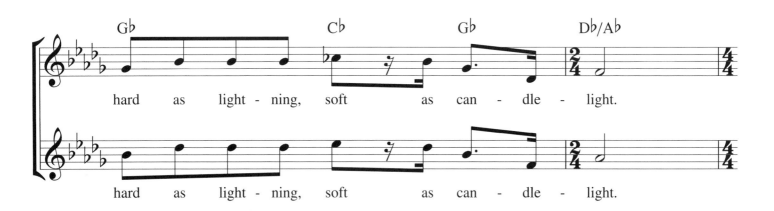

hard as light-ning, soft as can-dle-light.

hard as light-ning, soft as can-dle-light.

Close your

Dare you trust the mu-sic of the night?

Bridge

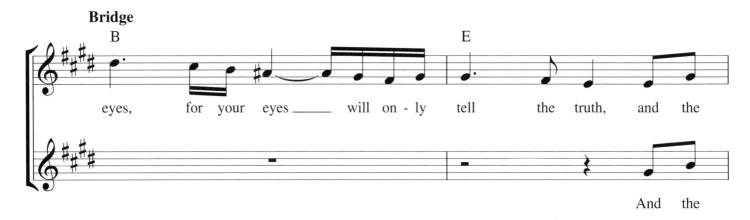

eyes, for your eyes _____ will on-ly tell the truth, and the

And the

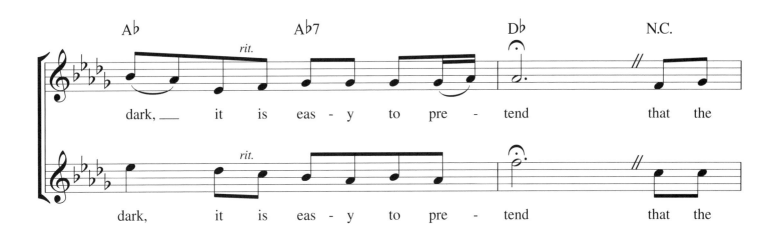

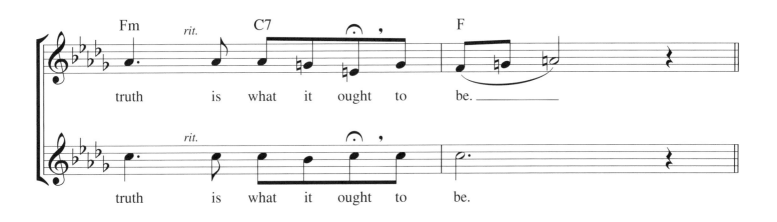

Verse

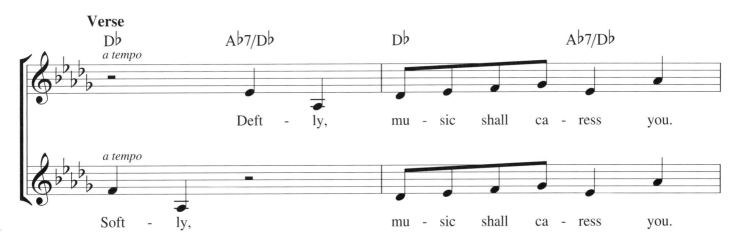

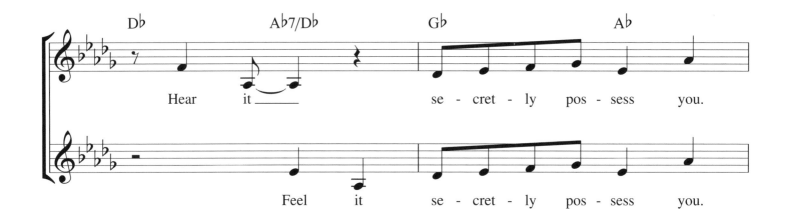

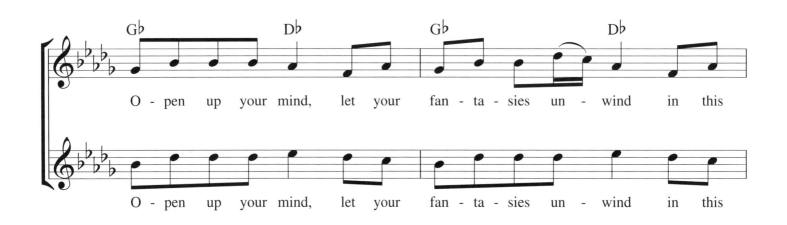

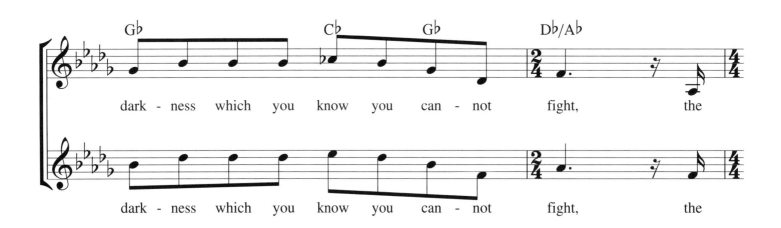

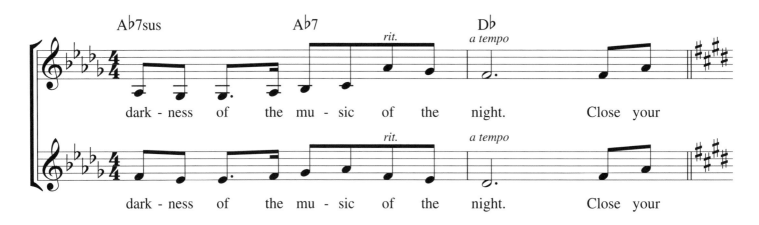

Bridge

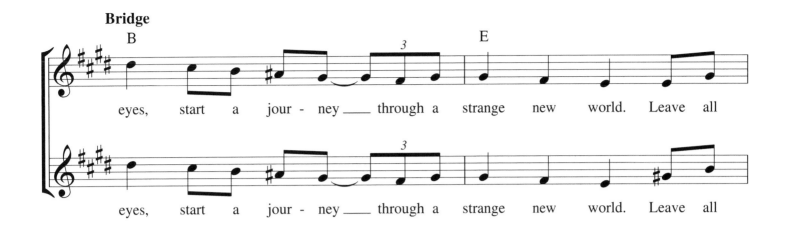

eyes, start a jour - ney _____ through a strange new world. Leave all

eyes, start a jour - ney _____ through a strange new world. Leave all

thoughts of the world you knew be - fore. Close your

thoughts of the world you knew be - fore. Close your

eyes, _____ and let mu - sic set you _____ free. On - ly

eyes, and let mu - sic set you free. On - ly

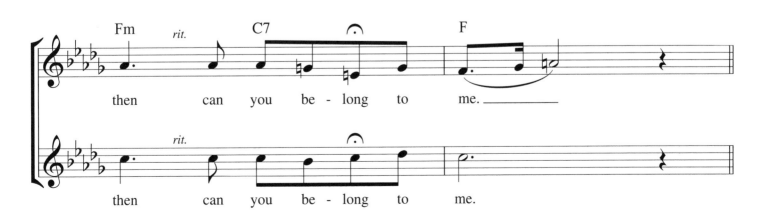

then can you be - long to me. _____

then can you be - long to me.

Verse

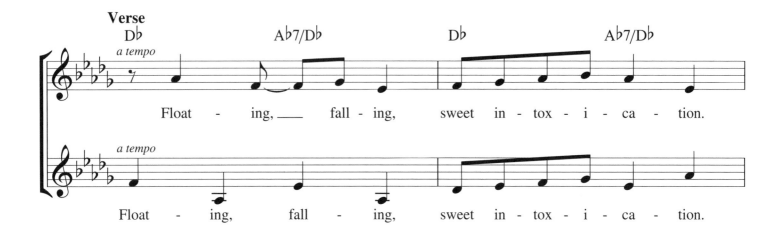

Float - ing, ___ fall - ing, sweet in - tox - i - ca - tion.

Float - ing, fall - ing, sweet in - tox - i - ca - tion.

Touch me, trust me, sa - vor each sen - sa - tion.

Touch me, trust me, sa - vor each sen - sa - tion.

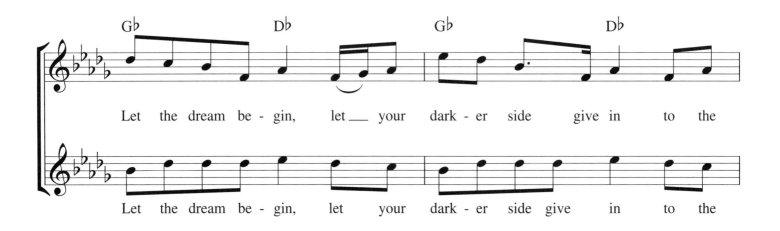

Let the dream be - gin, let __ your dark - er side give in to the

Let the dream be - gin, let your dark - er side give in to the

pow - er of the mu - sic that I write, the

pow - er of the mu - sic that I write, the

Shall We Dance?

from THE KING AND I

Lyrics by Oscar Hammerstein II
Music by Richard Rodgers

Intro
Brightly

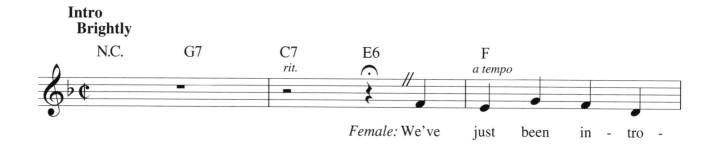

Female: We've just been in-tro-

duced.   I   do   not   know   you   well,   but

when   the   mus-ic   start-ed,   some-thing   drew   me   to   your

side.   So   man-y   men   and   girls   are

in   each   oth-er's   arms,   it   made   me   think

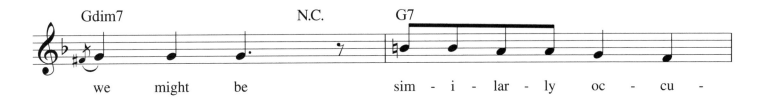

we might be   sim - i - lar - ly oc - cu -

Chorus

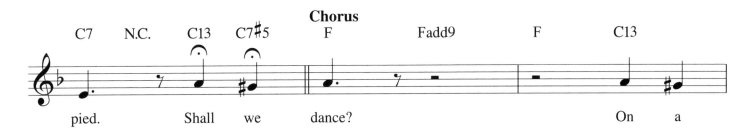

pied.   Shall we dance?   On a

bright cloud of mu - sic, shall we fly?

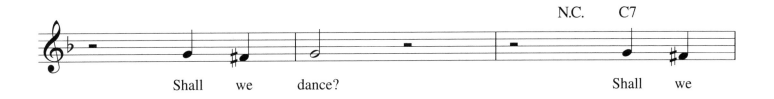

Shall we dance?   Shall we

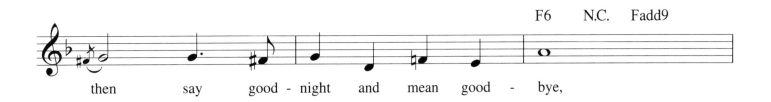

then say good - night and mean good - bye,

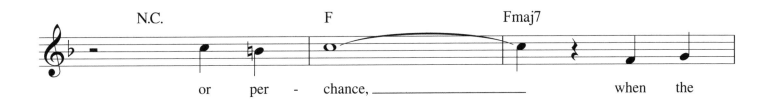

or per - chance, _____ when the

last lit - tle star has left the sky,

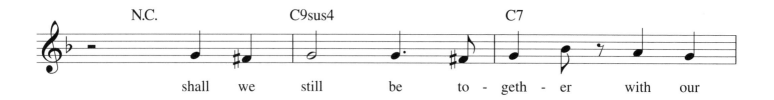

shall we still be to - geth - er with our

arms a - round each oth - er, and shall you be my

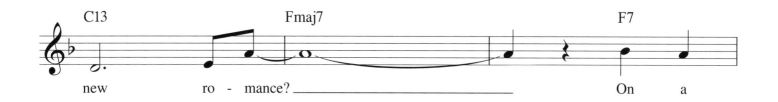

new ro - mance? _____ On a

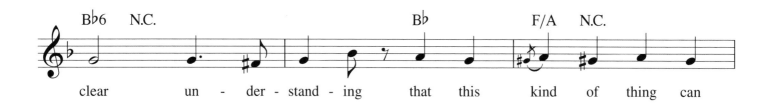

clear un - der - stand - ing that this kind of thing can

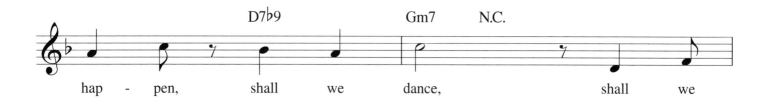

hap - pen, shall we dance, shall we

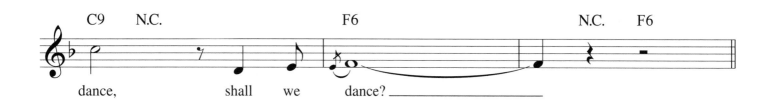

dance, shall we dance? _____

Interlude

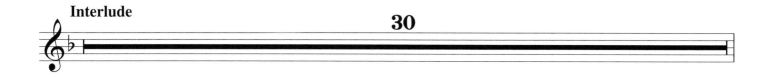

30

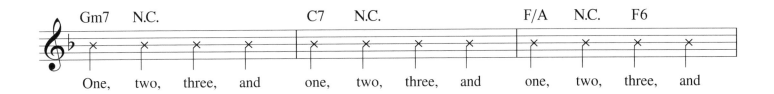

One, two, three, and one, two, three, and one, two, three, and

Chorus

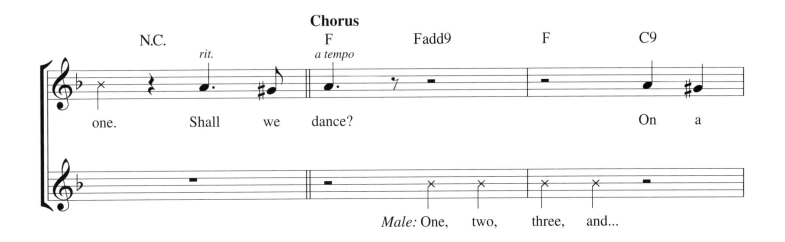

one. Shall we dance? On a

Male: One, two, three, and...

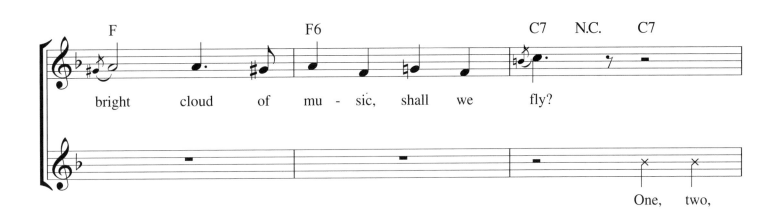

bright cloud of mu - sic, shall we fly?

One, two,

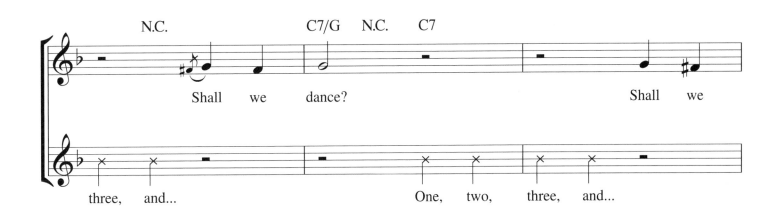

Shall we dance? Shall we

three, and... One, two, three, and...

then say good - night and mean good - bye?

One, two,

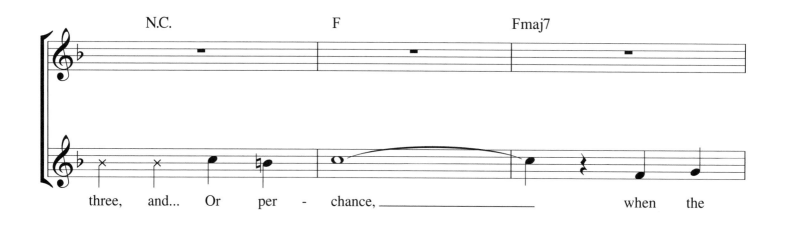

three, and... Or per - chance, _____ when the

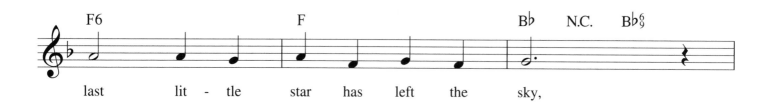

last lit - tle star has left the sky,

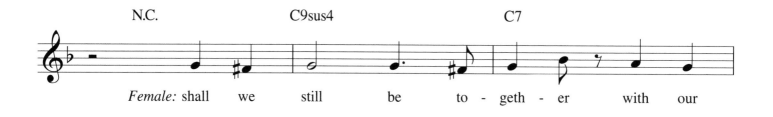

Female: shall we still be to - geth - er with our

arms a - round each oth - er, and shall you be my

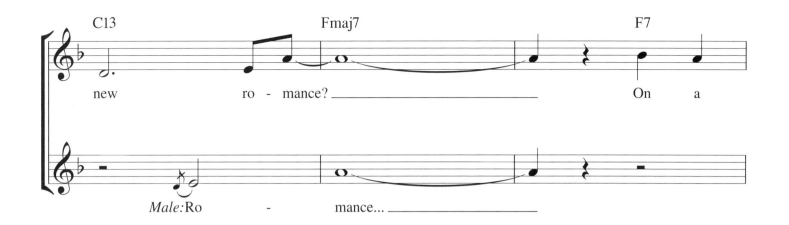

new ro - mance? _____ On a

Male: Ro - mance... _____

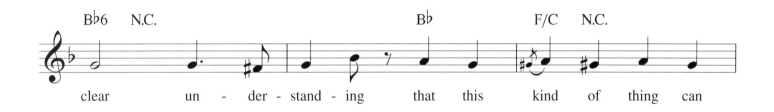

clear un - der - stand - ing that this kind of thing can

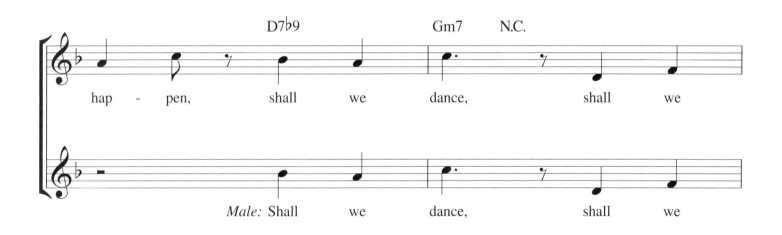

hap - pen, shall we dance, shall we

Male: Shall we dance, shall we

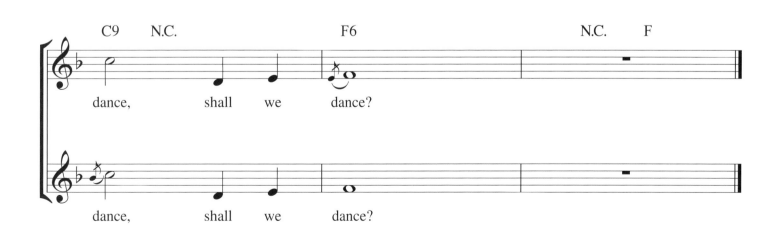

dance, shall we dance?

dance, shall we dance?

Some Enchanted Evening

from SOUTH PACIFIC
Lyrics by Oscar Hammerstein II
Music by Richard Rodgers

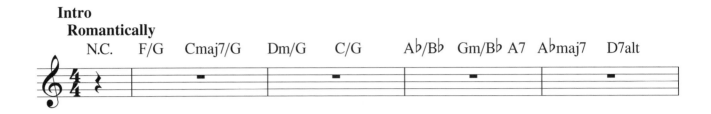

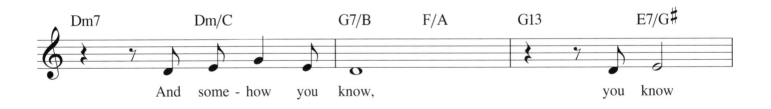

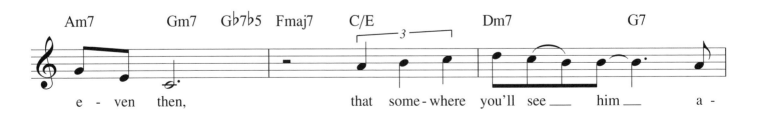

Speak Low

from the Musical Production ONE TOUCH OF VENUS
Words by Ogden Nash
Music by Kurt Weill

Intro
Relaxed Smooth-Jazz groove

Verse

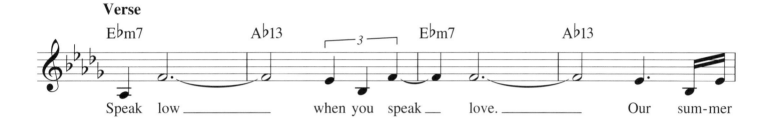

Speak low ____ when you speak ____ love. ____ Our sum-mer

day with-ers a-way too ____ soon, ____ too __

__ soon. ____ Speak low ____ when you speak __

__ love. ____ Our mo-ment is swift. Like ships a-

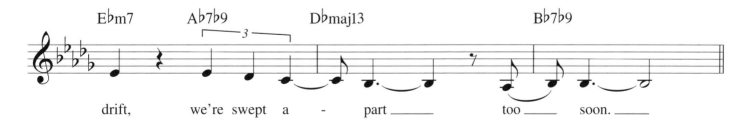

drift, we're swept a-part ____ too __ soon. ____

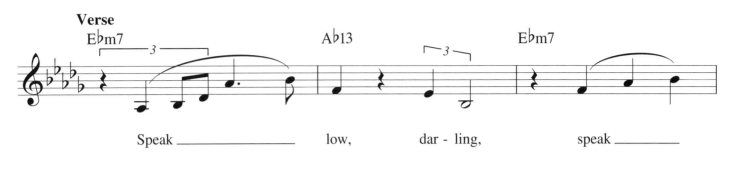

Verse

Speak _____ low, dar - ling, speak _____

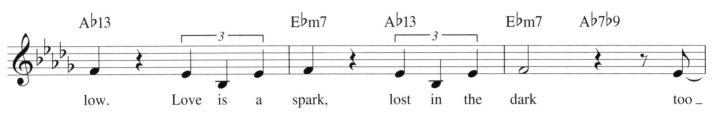

low. Love is a spark, lost in the dark too _

____ soon, _____ too _____ soon. _____ I feel, _____

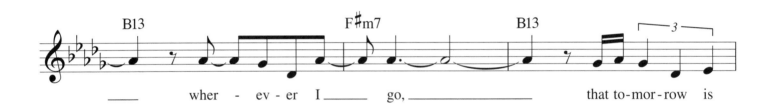

____ wher - ev - er I _____ go, _____ that to - mor - row is

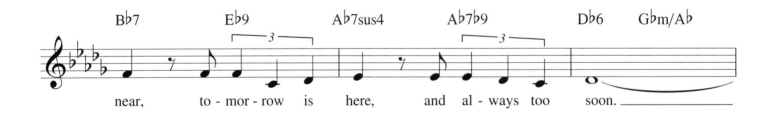

near, to - mor - row is here, and al - ways too soon. ____

Bridge

____ Time _____ is _____ so old, ___

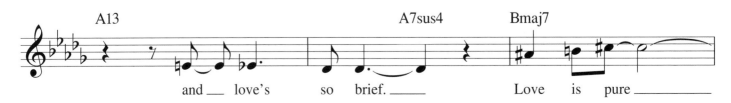

and _ love's so brief. ____ Love is pure _____

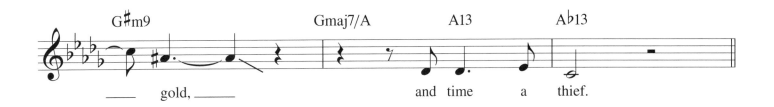

G#m9   Gmaj7/A   A13   Ab13

___ gold, ___   and time   a   thief.

Verse

Ebm7   Ab13   Ebm7

We're ___ late, _____ dar - ling,   we're ___ late. _____

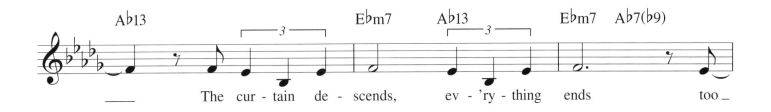

Ab13   Ebm7   Ab13   Ebm7   Ab7(b9)

___ The cur - tain de - scends, ev - 'ry - thing ends   too ___

Fm7b5   Bb7b9   F#m7

___ soon, _____ too ___ soon. _____ I ___ wait, _____

B13   F7b5   B7b5   Ab/Bb   Bb7b9

___ dar - ling, ___ I ___ wait. _____ Will you speak

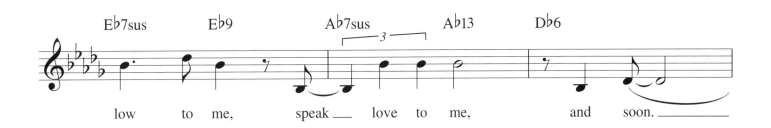

Eb7sus   Eb9   Ab7sus   Ab13   Db6

low   to me,   speak ___ love to me,   and   soon. ___

Interlude

Bb7b9   **7**   Bb7b9

___   I _____